A Baby Born in Faith and Love

My Baptism Memory Book

Beth Branigan McNamara

Contributing Author
Gina Wright McKeever
Illustrated by Brenda Anderson
Design by Kathi Hilaski

Our Sunday Visitor Publishing Division
Our Sunday Visitor, Inc.
Huntington, Indiana 46750

Editorial consultant: Alfred McBride, O. Praem.

Our Sunday Visitor Publishing Division
Our Sunday Visitor, Inc.
200 Noll Plaza
Huntington, IN 46750

International Standard Book Number: 0-87973-367-5

Cover and inside design by: Kathi Hilaski
Illustrations by: Brenda Anderson

PRINTED IN THE UNITED STATES OF AMERICA

367

Remembering Cherished Moments

A Keepsake for:

____

Given With Love From:

____

In the Year of Our Lord:

____

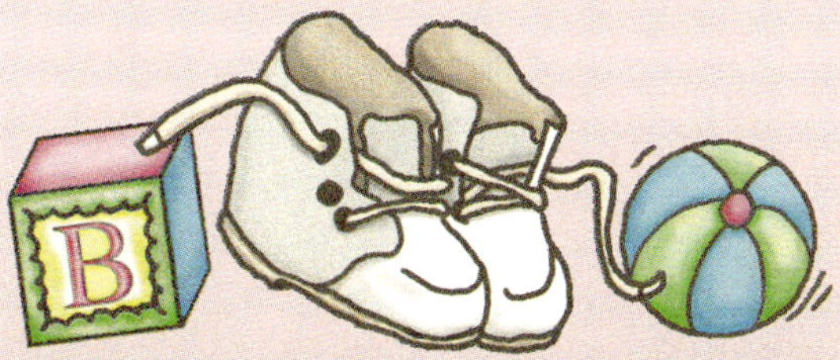

Dear Parents,

From the love you have for each other, God has called forth this beautiful creation. God has a deep and eternal love for you and your child. With God's help, you will nurture, care for, and love this child. As you watch your child grow and experience new things in life, your faith in God and yourself will be affirmed.

The following pages will be filled with treasured memories of your child's beginnings. Record the events of your child's young life and share your thoughts, faith, and dreams. What a joyful privilege it is to become a parent.

–Beth Branigan McNamara

Table of Contents

Our Thoughts Before You Arrived...

You knit me in my mother's womb.
Psalm 139:13

When we heard you were coming, we felt...

This is how we waited and prepared...

We want to share with you what we value in our lives…

PHOTO

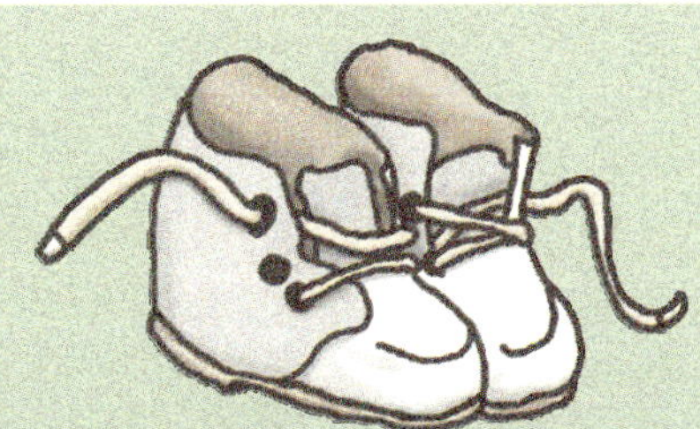

Thankful are we, loving God,
for this precious gift of life.

We Welcomed You Into Our Lives…

On

TIME WEEKDAY DATE YEAR

In

HOSPITAL CITY STATE

When we first saw you…

For everything there is a season,
and a time for every matter under heaven.
Ecclesiastes 3:1 (NRSV)

Your life was a gift,
a miracle from God's hands,
given at just the right time to touch lives
and fill hearts with the joy and love you bring.

PHOTO

You were greeted by…

Choosing the Right Name…

Names we considered…

The name we chose for you

We chose your name because…

A saint whose name you share, or who we have asked to watch over you

Is known for…

And whose feast day is celebrated

…Thus says the LORD…
"I have called you by name:
you are mine."
Isaiah 43:1

Welcoming You Home...

Our address

____

____

____

PHOTO

That your eyes may be open night and day toward this house, the place of which you said, "My name shall be there."
I Kings 8:29 (NRSV)

Hush, little Baby,
How precious you are,
As you slumber so sweetly
Under God's stars.

PHOTO

Your favorite places to sleep are…

We Are Yo

The love and faith of gene

Grandfather's Father

BIRTHPLACE/DATE

Grandmother's Father

BIRTHPLACE/DATE

Grandfather's Mother

BIRTHPLACE/DATE

Grandmother's Mother

BIRTHPLACE/DATE

Grandfather

BIRTHPLACE/DATE

Grandmother

BIRTHPLACE/DATE

Father

BIRTHPLACE/DATE

Others who love and care for you
(siblings, aunts, uncles, friends)…

ur Family

tions is handed on to you.

Grandfather's Father

BIRTHPLACE/DATE

Grandmother's Father

BIRTHPLACE/DATE

Grandfather's Mother

BIRTHPLACE/DATE

Grandmother's Mother

BIRTHPLACE/DATE

Grandfather

BIRTHPLACE/DATE

Grandmother

BIRTHPLACE/DATE

Mother

BIRTHPLACE/DATE

Child's First Middle Last Name

We decided to have you baptized because…

We prepared for your Baptism by…

God is the giver of all life. May God bless the parents of this child. They will be the first teachers of their child in the way of the faith. May they also be the best of teachers, bearing witness to the faith by what they do and say.

Rite of Baptism
(paraphrased)

We have asked

____

and

____

To be your Godparents because…

____

____

____

____

DATE

Dear Godchild,

____

____

____

____

____

____

Your Godfather,

____

____

DATE

Dear Godchild,

____

____

____

____

____

____

Your Godmother,

____

You Were Baptized Into the Faith

…One Lord, one faith, one baptism;
one God and Father of all…
Ephesians 4:5-6

The day of your Baptism was memorable because…

We will always remember…

...keep the light of Christ
burning brightly in your heart.
Rite of Baptism

PHOTO

The friends and relatives who celebrated your Baptism with us...

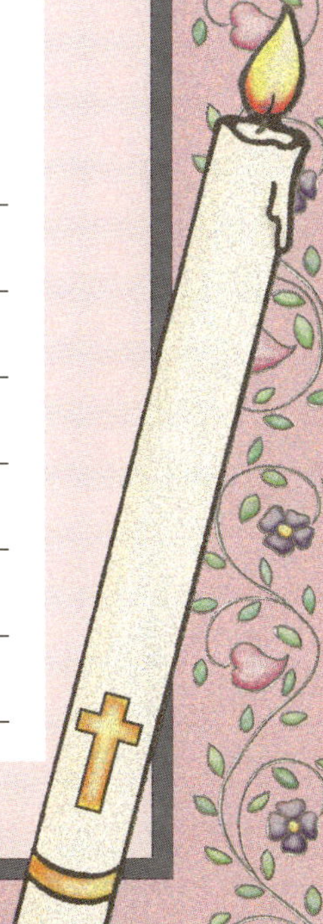

Record of Baptism

Child

____

Of

____

NAME OF PARENTS

Born on

____

MONTH DAY YEAR

In

____

CITY, STATE

Was Baptized

____

CHILD'S NAME

In the Name of the Father,
Son, and Holy Spirit

On

____

MONTH DAY YEAR

By

____

PRIEST/DEACON

At the Catholic Church of

____

Located in

____

CITY, STATE

Godparents

____

Our prayer for you…

Love, your parents,

We Are Your Church...

The Catholic community of

____

NAME OF PARISH

PHOTO

*We are part of a large community filled with faith,
hope, and love. The Church spans centuries,
extending her open arms to all who
choose to embrace God's love.*

Welcome wishes and messages from our community…

From our priest (deacon)…

From our parish members and friends…

We Celebrate

The ordinary moment

First Full Night of Sleep…

First Recognizes Mother

Rolls Over

First Recognizes Father

First Haircut

Favorite Foods

Your Life. . .

hat become special times.

First Tooth

First Steps

First Words

Favorite Toys

Drinks From a Cup

Pets

Your First

Bless this child's first birthday.
Bless the nights with restful sleep.
Bless the days and joyful play.
Watch this child grow in heart and mind.
Bless this little love of mine.

PHOTO

We celebrated by…

Birthday...

Family and friends who celebrated with us...

____

____

____

____

____

PHOTO

A year of new beginnings
is about to pass before our eyes.
Dreams of the days yet to come.
God's work of art is never done.

Prayers to Say

Sign of the Cross

In the name of Father,
and of the Son,
and of the Holy Spirit.
Amen.

Grace

Bless us, O Lord, and these your gifts,
which we are about to receive from
your bounty,
through Christ our Lord.
Amen.

Guardian Angel Prayer

Angel of God, my guardian dear,
To whom his love commits me here,
Ever this day be at my side,
To light and guard, to rule and guide.
Amen.

and Keep . . .

Glory Be

Glory be to the Father,
and to the Son,
and to the Holy Spirit.
As it was in the beginning, is now,
and ever shall be,
world without end.
Amen.

Hail Mary

Hail, Mary, full of grace;
the Lord is with thee;
Blessed art thou among
women and blessed is the
fruit of thy womb, Jesus.
Holy Mary, Mother of God,
pray for us sinners, now and at
the hour of our death.
Amen.

Prayers to Say

Our Father,

Our Father, who art in heaven,
hallowed be thy name.
Thy kingdom come;
Thy will be done on earth as it is in heaven.
Give us this day our daily bread;
and forgive us our trespasses as we forgive
those who trespass against us;
and lead us not into temptation,
but deliver us from evil.
Amen.

and Keep...

Wake Up Prayer

Thank you, God, for this day.
Another day to learn and play.
With giggles and wiggles,
My love I send
Help me, God, to be a good friend.
Amen.

Good Night Prayer

The night has come, it's time for bed.
I close my eyes as I rest my head.
Thank you, God, for this great day.
You know how much I like to play.
As you watch me from above,
I'll see your stars glow with love.
Amen.

Your Second

God of life, bless this child.
Give these hands a gentle touch,
guide these eyes to see the sun
and fill this life with love and fun.

PHOTO

We celebrated by…

Birthday…

These were the people who shared the day with you…

PHOTO

This year sweet memories were made
As our family laughed and played,
All the while hardly knowing
Just how much our love was growing.

Holi

Are h

What we will

Your First Christmas…

First Easter…

First Thanksgiving…

ays...
days.

ember about...

Other Treasured Times...

PHOTO

Families gather around the table
joining hands and hearts.

Your Third

May God bless your eyes with a sparkle
and fill your smile with giggles and glee.
God bless you as you bounce and jump for joy
becoming the person you were meant to be.
God bless you as you celebrate being three.

PHOTO

We celebrated by…

Birthday…

These were the people who shared the day with you…

PHOTO

Your small steps have led to new skills,
With our praise, encouragement, and love.
You are using your gifts from God above.

Celebrating God's Presence in Your Life…

The sacraments of initiation—
Baptism, Eucharist, and Confirmation—
form the foundation of Christian faith.

PHOTO

You received your First Eucharist on

____

MONTH DAY YEAR

At the Church of

____

From

____

CELEBRANT

You Received Confirmation

On

MONTH DAY YEAR

At the Church of

From

CELEBRANT

PHOTO

I am the light of the world. Whoever follows me will not walk in darkness but will have the light of life.
John 8:12

A Letter From Your Parents

Dear

We want you to remember…

We love you!

There will always be a prayer for you in our hearts.